This book belongs

Samiyah

ISBN 0-7172-8283-X

Jim Henson's
Muppet Babies
Count
with Me

by Louise Gikow   illustrated by David Prebenna

GROLIER

1 One Muppet Baby
hopping up and down.

Two Muppet Babies climbing all around.

2

3 Three Muppet Babies painting and sewing.

Four Muppet Babies
swimming and rowing.

4

5 Five Muppet Babies
slipping down a slide.

Six Muppet Babies
going for a ride.

6

7

Seven Muppet Babies
dancing and singing.

8

Eight Muppet Babies
laughing and swinging.

9

Nine Muppet Babies
making mud pies.

10

Ten Muppet Babies
all in disguise.

You've counted Muppet Babies
from one to ten.
Now, take a deep breath...
and do it again!